The Godspell Solution

The Godspell Solution

an extraordinary dialog with a voice of God

on

Life, Love, Healing & Abundance

by Bill Jason O'Mara

Granite Publishing, LLC
P.O. Box 1429
Columbus, NC 28722

Library of Congress Cataloging-in-Publication Data

O'Mara, Bill Jason, 1962-
    The godspell solution : on life, love, acceptance & creation, spiced with fun, healing,
    and radical abundance / by Bill Jason O'Mara.
        p. cm.

ISBN 1-893183-20-3

1. Spiritual life. 2. Conduct of life. 3 Imaginary conversations. I. Title.

BL624.O45 1999
291.4'4--dc21   99-057380

Cover Artwork: Suzanne Maksel
Manuscript editor: Amy Owen Demmon

Printed in the United States of America.

Address all inquiries to:
Granite Publishing, LLC
P. O. Box 1429
Columbus, NC 28722
U.S.A.

Granite Publishing, LLC, is committed
to using environmentally responsible paper.

Dear Reader:

My name is Bill. I'm a lot like you. I question why I'm here, what I should do, and what it's all about. I have spent most of my life asking these questions.

Today, through God's grace, I start on a journey similar to many. I have been asked by a deep voice inside to get on my computer and dictate the following book.

This may seem strange, yet, as a meditator, I have become accustomed to tapping into a voice now and then. At this moment, after doing some intense work on myself, the channel is clear. I release my ego to this Spirit Guide and say, "Okay, let it happen."

I send each of you many blessings. I feel lucky to be here, even though I spent most of my life cursing God for sending me. This is a new journey for me—one of tenderness and open heart. I pray that this journey and these words will bless you. *KJai Bhagwan.*

Bill Jason O'Mara
Encinitas, California
October 16, 1997

Acknowledgements

Cori,

Carmella,

all the Miracle students everywhere,

and, of course, George.

Additional thanks to:

— Pam & Brian (publishers) Way to go! Thank you!

—Wayne Dyer, Marianne Williamson and James Redfield

—Mom, Dad, Shari, Mike and all the Gang!

Day by Day

Day by Day

Oh Dear Lord

3 things I pray

to see thee more clearly

to love thee more dearly

to follow thee more nearly

Day by Day by Day by Day!

Written by
Stephen Schwartz

table of contents

1) *love*
10-16-97

Dear Spirit, what is your name?

My name is George. I am a voice of God. I want you to think of me as a humble man, a man you probably wouldn't even notice. I am often dressed as a street person in disheveled attire. Please look at me.

I do not understand: George?

Yes, George.

Why a humble man? I have so often thought of you as a great king on some throne somewhere.

It is true that I have a throne. The throne is on the street, on the beach, wherever life takes me. I am alive as you are. In truth I say that I am a voice of God, for I am more than any voice. I am the spirit wind, the tree that feeds you oxygen and brings you shade. I am Mother Earth and Father Sky. I speak to the trees through the sun. I speak to the fish through water. I speak to you through love. If love is hard to hear, you'll hear a voice. That's all.

Why have you come to me?

For the simple reason that you have been told for years to relax, to play, to lighten up, to stop fretting about this dream called life. Too many are fretting, and, thus, too few are awakening. I think you are a good student. Why *not* you?

All right. What is awakening?

Awakening is the call to *realize who you really are.* It is the love this chapter alludes to. And, of course, once you know, you laugh at all this earthly drama and chase after self-esteem through "externalitis." For I am all things in nature, and if all of humanity is "I am," as the holy books state, then who am I but you? And you are me—love. Every earthly drama is in direct proportion to the extent that people don't realize their identity.

Look at the shift in the last few years—books like *Return to Love, Embraced by the Light,* and more. Millions of people seeking spiritual truth. We have come to a time of choice—play more or forever live in numb depression. Easy choice, huh? And know, this "new age" is only the old age revisited, for there is no time—only *readiness,* a readiness that moves us to awaken. How long must we be stressed until we say, "Maybe I'll try de-stress."

So, okay, a lot is coming out, but what is love?

Love is simply the awareness of the interconnection of it all. Once we sit still long enough to listen to our own voice, to see the beauty of nature, of wind, trees, and water, we begin to shift our priorities. We ask, "I know there has got to be something more than the small difficult life I'm leading." This is when love begins. Love is not a romantic notion of affection for someone else. It's the *absolute bliss* that arises when you are alone, *feeling* the harmony and perfection of it all, that all of existence is connected and perfect. It is in those moments that we realize that only our fear destroys the perfection.

Okay, I think I'm getting this. So why is there fear? This bothers me so. I was taught that God was all powerful. So I've spent most of my

life mad that there is bad, evil, and fear in the world. Why are there starving people? Why is there AIDS? Why is there war and cruelty?

The answer is a very simple one, one you have heard before but have been reluctant to believe. The truth is that love and fear are energies on opposite ends of the same stick. Most humans, however, perceive "love" in this sense as a need to obtain approval. Whereas fear is the perception that there are pains to be avoided. Both love and fear create deep emotional disturbance—a chase to obtain or avoid something to make it better. The real pain, we will discover, is only our separation from spirit.

This is very different than love, which is much greater than either of these emotions. Love is not an emotion. It is the only *true* universal feeling. Fear is the quest for the self-defeating, the self-destruction that comes from not knowing love. Thus, if you grab the stick called life you receive both fear and false love, until we step out of it. The trick is, so to speak, to embrace both ends of the stick while on Earth and rise to the God within. God, in this respect, requires a sense of humor. Yes, humor. God requires that inner smile that is above it all. Then we can see the perfection in the imperfection. Thus, if we all know who we are, and some disaster happens to trigger fear, we can choose a new response. The focus on the stick brings anguish, pain, destruction. What can one do other than curse the heavens? I say this—grab both ends of the stick. Find your spiritual sense of humor—there is a place inside of you that is bigger than both these earthly emotions—and choose the love in spite of the fear or the erroneous sense of love that was handed you.

This is a big step. When all hell is around you, what do you do? Do you become the hell or become the heaven? The miracle of life is that there is so much love to overcome the stick. Why play with the stick of emotions? That is why the angels have told Dannion Brinkley, and countless others, to create stress centers to get our fellow brothers and sisters out of the collective malaise of the status-quo chase for fear emotions, the seduction of suffering. If we don't de-stress, we can never rise to this higher place of love. Now, more than ever, the angels are here in force to say, "it is time." Today, my friends, choose to get past the emotions of false love and fear.

Wow, that was a lot. So what you are saying is, in some sense, that good and evil, or love and fear, are just energies that exist. You can't create the one without the other.

Yes, this exists everywhere in nature: the food chain, life and death, sleep and awake, eating and digestion. There are opposites around us continually. Why do we fight the inherent nature of it all? Maybe we don't want the disease, or the death, or to be eaten. Of course, these events appear scary. Yet, they are *natural*. When you think of it, what one calls bad, or fear, is nothing more than their perception of what they don't want, yet, in another sense, have chosen. Acceptance of "what is," is what I call the spiritual sense of humor. This is the flow of life; enjoy it for all its absurdity. How many of our Earth brothers and sisters spend countless hours cursing God for "what is" as if it should be different. I say to you, when you realize who you really are, this mindset will change. When you *know* you are love, then life events become more harmonic, less painful and unpredictable. And when the inevitable "bad" thing happens, we in a higher sense can rejoice, for the natural progression of life and death is progressing as nature dictates. Without this progression life would cease. So, my friends, please know it is okay to mourn and to be angry at certain injustices. Go into that completely and reach the other side. Please don't repress the inner turmoil. It needs to come up so one can move on. My prayer for you is the one I have for myself and all the angels. In spite of the surroundings or the events, take the step. Sit in life with this stick in hand and, at the same time, you are God: Great, Omnipresent, Divine. Enjoy the journey.

I'm sorry. I had to leave for a moment. They are replacing my roof today and my house is in shambles. Also, I want to tell you what a strange experience this channeling is for me. I feel out of control, like

4

what is coming out is all over the place and is breaking all the rules of writing. I guess this is beyond all that.

Yes, my friend. I will call you Willy affectionately. I hope you like that.

Yes, that is fine. I've never been a Willy to anyone but you and my Uncle Mike.

Yes, Michael likes your fun spirit.

Okay, is there any more you want me to write in this chapter?

Only this: Life is a powerful experience with many sides and paradoxes. The ability to go beyond the mundane and see the perfection—the spiritual peace in accepting "what is"—is very freeing. And, paradoxically, while we are accepting what is, we are also creating peace on Earth through helping others de-stress as well. This is love because ultimately our inner peace and understanding, our very existence, comes from a bipolar focus on acceptance and creation. From this warrior commitment to acceptance and creation, the heart grows with love and compassion for self and all others. So, you might say that *the discipline of acceptance and creation is what brings the feeling of love.*

So, Willy, I say goodbye for today. Do not attempt to fully comprehend all that has been given to you on this day. Enjoy. Keep your spiritual sense of humor and move on with compassion for this day, as many have not grasped this perspective and are in great pain. Offer your heart as you can and move forward as a divine angel warrior of the universal love. Bless you for this day. I will talk to you and give you a chapter each day for nine days. On the tenth day, I will tell you who to contact and what to send. Leave the rest up to me. When we are compensated for our work here together, please divide our earnings into thirds:

1) play,

2) stress center,

3) spirit family.

I'll fill in the rest later. Love to you, my friend. Thank you for getting started.

George and the angel gang. Good day.

Thoughts to play with:

I am God.

Love is the only Feeling.

Accept life as it is: humor and divine order.

Something to do:

Keep an eye out for a counselor or workshop that feels right and can support you on your journey to self-realization, to help you de-stress.

Self-realization is not something you get, it is something you accept.

Contemplations...

love

2) *who am I?*
10-18-97

Dear Spirit, George, I am very tired today. I find that writing this totally exhausts me. Can you offer me some help?

Yes, my friend, release the judgment. You are like many, you ask, "Why me?" You feel not worthy, so you say, "This isn't God speaking. This is some insane sinister ego-voice trying to get one over on people." Now this is a wonderful segue into our chapter today, isn't it?

Yes, it sounds like it.

Let me tell you, as I said before: If we knew who we really were on the Earth plane, pain would be impossible. There would be less of the "unpredictable" that so many fear; harmony and understanding would reign. Instead of someone getting a cold and saying, "Drat, another bleeping cold," their deeper understanding of who they are would respond to the perfection of the cold. The cold is helping release the unneeded energy in the body. Thus, there is no wrong—only perfect synchronicity.

Yes, I get it. But I can't help but go back to the many who are starving, those who have been raped, shot at, etc. Certainly I can't look them in the eye and tell them, "This is in divine order. This is what your body needs to release negative energy."

Well, Willy, I sense your frustration. It goes back to the stick analogy we spoke of before. We imagine what is "love," what is "right," and what is "pleasurable," and from that we start a chase. At the same time, we have an image of what is "bad," "wrong," and to be "avoided," like sickness, rape, injury—and from that we start to run away. Who is to say what a soul may need? The soul has chosen. Let it experience it—acceptance and creation. The only way "out," so to speak, is to take the step up. Accept with a sense of humor the harmonic progression, and simultaneously create a soulful life where you are. The questions people really want answers to are, "Why do XYZ terrible things happen?" "What can I do to prevent them?" "Why me?"

I say, they do not happen to you. You have called them for your soul's perfection. You can't prevent them because you want them. And "Why me?" is because this is the destiny of all souls in quest of their divine self, their spirit.

Yes, George, but it sounds so matter of fact, like it doesn't hurt.

I understand, Willy. The truth is it hurts a lot less than continued alienation from your own spirit. Think of all the millions who have discovered who they really are because something "out of the ordinary" came and threw a wrench in their "pleasant" progression of life. These are everyday occurrences from minor to major events: death, divorce, disease, violence, addiction, bankruptcy, getting fired, moving, disconnection from others, getting fed up, etc.

This is the journey of life. If life catered to your every whim, it is quite possible you would continue to drift away from your own spirit. That is why every spiritual book ever written always alludes to: those who are last shall be first; seek first the kingdom; detach from worldly obsession, and so on. That which we obsess about as being "right" or "wrong" keeps us from getting close to our heaven, our inner peace, our spirit. This is suffering!

And please note this is a forgiving universe. There is compassion and love surrounding each of our brothers and sisters. No one is left alone. This you must believe from your own intuitive knowing, for I am certain there are times where you "think" you are alone and abandoned. You are not. For now, please tap into this one thought: It's all in divine order; you are safe. The quicker "I" adapt this as my theme of life, the quicker "I" will accept my circumstances with glee and move on to create more love on the Earth. As long as one is stuck on the treadmill of "Why me?"; "What can I do to protect myself?"; "Who do I complain to?"; they can never move forward, out of the collective malaise of brainwashed externalist suffering.

Wow, that's a mouth full. I don't know if I can follow this all....

Just know this, my friend. Each of you reading has a place, a practice, and a way of undoing, of relaxing, of being, of quitting the brainwashed mind. In this silence, the light of truth emerges. *You don't have to learn through pain. You can relax.* It may be in yoga or painting, in biking or lying on the beach, in sex or whatever. In your special silence, you sense a deep synchronistic truth—that all that has happened, and will happen, is taking you closer and closer to perfect love. Of course, you *are* perfect love already. Yet, it is our unknowing of this that makes the journey of life occur. So, my friends, rejoice. Be still. See the higher perfection of it all. This is your time to shine, to accept and to create the imaginable utopia you have always wanted—a utopia of peace, not one of endless satisfaction of ego desire, but of love, peace, and harmony with self and others. Now is the time. The universe is speeding up its paradoxical ways. Now more than ever there is confusion. The forces of union and separation are working overtime. Please join the angels in helping yourself, and all our brothers and sisters, find union. There is no more time for the stick addiction.

I say, keep this thought in mind: *You don't have to do what you think you have to do.* In fact, you may need to do the exact opposite. Try it. Get naked. Lighten up. Go play. Stop working. Be outrageous. Do nothing. Now is the time. This is what we all want anyway—to play. So why do we continue plodding through life spending 99% of our waking hours participating in things we hate? I say this: quit, revolt, live somewhere else. Do anything that nurtures you and de-stresses you. Do not fear. *The sacred spirit inside you will always find a way to feed and take care of all your needs.* There is always a way. Just remember to clarify, "What is my truest need?" A house? A Mercedes? A million dollars? There is nothing wrong with any of these possessions (that you can't possess). They are neutral, meaningless. Until one has taken the step, to accept who he or she is, these items often trap one into more ego, more work, more stress, more fear, and more Stu Wilde "ticktockness" to protect themselves from the stuff going away. Thanks, Stu!

Okay, I'm overwhelmed. Can you answer why you keep saying we?

Thank you for asking. The truth is I am no different than you. If you really grasped this, you would never curse me. I created the energy and with that energy comes the light and the dark, the up and the down, the left and right, the inhale and exhale, *and* the choice to be free or a victim! Throughout eternity the challenge is, which will you live by? At any moment any of us could choose either: freedom or victimhood. The angels of light and I are clear of the eternal pain that the darkness emits. So, it is easy for us to make the choice for light. It's not always easy to keep, but one worth staying committed to.

You mean, you struggle with light and dark like we do?

Yes, that is why I have asked the spirit guides to talk to you as older brothers and sisters who have been through it, too. You know, it is hard to connect with someone, even a guide or angel, if you believe him to be different than you. The truth is that no being is different. We have all struggled through the same confrontations, the same choices. Now we send our love through this book, and through a million different means, to remind our earthly brothers and sisters of their path and their need to stay open to us. When you have an older brother offering a helping hand, why not take it?

OK, slow down. Let me ask some questions. What about the darkness? Victimhood? What about "the step"? Is there a first step or many steps?

Yes, you want to know why I created darkness and fear, why there are victims, and so on. I say, I create energy as you do every moment. This energy has two poles. At any moment you are *free* to choose which pole of energy you choose to live in. If there were no poles, there would be no freedom. And if there were no freedom, there would be no life. We would all be robots. Yes, it may be frustrating to acknowledge these two energies. So I ask you a question: "Do you enjoy freedom, or would you prefer the confines of a metal robot shell that has no free choice, only thoughts given to him?" This is always the question I receive: "Why? Why? Why?" So I want you to hear this: Freedom has its costs. The costs are not always easy to pay for (i.e.: to eat, one must kill some living thing). Nature is filled with these choices of freedom. I say, do not curse the choice, for *no choice* is always more harming to the soul.

I don't understand.

Let me explain it this way. You are part of me. Each of you are all beings—the planet, the trees, and the great sea are nothing but cells in my body—just like you have cells in your body that do their thing. When the cells in your body separate and alienate, there is cancer. When the human soul separates and alienates, it, too, becomes a cancer to itself and to the Universe. It all is connected. We each gain freedom together or cancer together. So it does not matter what you call it, be it love and fear, freedom and victimhood, light or darkness. They are just energies to choose from. We all know when we live on the love side we feel free: free, connected, and alive. It's a wonderful place.

To sum up, the soul is questing, seeking answers. It doesn't know it is a cell in God's body. It doesn't know that it is already perfect. Thus, it goes about trying to discover who it is, where it is, and so forth—a cosmic search fueled by freedom that leads to only one conclusion. Stop the

13

search. Simply look around and realize who you are. *Stop.* Get quiet. Slow down. De-stress. Let the freedom take you home.

The challenge for the soul is this realization may take a long "time" in happening because there is a part of you that still wants the pain, a part of you that wants to suffer and do "time" for your "sin" of supposed separation. This "time" by Earth standards may mean lifetimes. For example, in one life you were a king who controlled many people, the next a slave who suffered great torture, the next a warrior who killed, and so on. The soul tries on every pair of pants until it stops the quest. Only the fearful separate self-quests. The soul, then, must only realize that it is not a separate ego, but that it is infinite spirit. The perfect being that has nothing to do and no where to go—just bliss. Finding God, then, always comes from getting fed up. I bet you know this!

So, stop the quest, realize who you are. A thousand times an hour remind yourself, *"I am a holy child of God, perfectly whole and complete in every way. I need do nothing. I need no one to validate me. I need only to open up, accept God's guidance, love myself and give my love to everyone I meet. I need only to create beauty in everything I do."* No other practice will bring as much joy. Accept and create. Accept the harmony that we all deserve within this sacred body of God. Create heaven on Earth.

Thanks. Please say more about the stick. I'm not sure I get it.

Yes, I will end here for today. The stick is the duality that many have spoken of. The stick is the ego—a separate part, separate from the tree not knowing its connection to the tree. It runs off in all insane directions with no apparent purpose but its own protection. Again, the soul is discovering what doesn't work. The ego is always linked with the unrealized mind searching for appeasement, for pleasure or pain. And either way, whether you get pleasure or pain, you are not happy. This is because the stick can never be satisfied until it reunites with the tree. The soul must awaken to its truth and release the ego mind.

So when I say, "Take a step"— the step of "self-realization"—you hold the stick tightly, raise your eyes to heaven, and say, "This ego-mind world stinks! What else is there?" because, under the ego conditions, it sure does. When you raise up and truly ask, "God, help, there's got to be another way," life truly begins. Follow this path. Listen. This is the outrageous phase: get rid of your stuff, sell the house, move somewhere new, and find the quiet, the beautiful, the nurturing. This is where it all begins. The rest is just shedding, like your dog once did. It is all release work, letting go of the brainwashing that you have bought into for centuries; chasing and running to or from lust, greed, materialism, weakness, etc. Searching for love—in all the wrong places!

You know what to do—yoga, body work, prayer, meditation, daily lessons from *A Course in Miracles*, walks in nature, being with awakened people, etc. Go live in an ashram.

For a time you will be in the intense shedding phase, then other phases will emerge. Once you have released, and have made a firm warrior decision to stay diligent in the realization, then you have accepted life. Now you can create. Now you are a fine-tuned angel of God, ready to spread love. Please hurry. Before this time, before your release, you can only create mayhem. If you doubt, try it and see. Go ahead - laugh.

Much love to all. Please de-stress. See you cats later.

George, Ashtar, Arcturus, Mahavishnu, and Fedrattrred.

Have a good day, Willy. See you later.

Thank you, God. I feel very touched today. For the first time in so long I feel your presence. I am so glad you are here with me. There is so much beauty when you look. Thank you for Godspell Solution; it helps me feel again. Praise you God. Love your loyal friend, Willy. Thank you for your love and trust in me. ...God, answer me one thing before we go. Why is there an ego?

This is the same as the question "Why is there fear?" These are energies, choices. They are available to anyone who wants to play with them. If someone wants to be an ego, they can. Then, 1000 years later, they discover it's not all that fun and they want to go home. So, as we reach the new millennium a lot of souls are saying, "Okay, I'm ready to stop this game. I'm tired of being so far away from who I really am."

Amen.

Good night, Willy. See you mañana!

Thoughts to play with:

All is in divine order. I am safe.

You don't have to do what you think you have to do.

Accept (I love me, I am healing me) and Create (I Share love, I help others heal).

I am not a victim—I am free.

Relax, go play, you are allowed.

Healing is relaxing, de-stressing, releasing the blocks to love.

Something to do:

Choose a daily discipline you can play with that helps you feel good, that helps you connect with your higher self, with the God within.

Suggestions: Prayer, Yoga, meditation, walks in nature....

Every morning, repeat the prayer:

"I am a holy child of God, perfectly whole and complete in every way. I need do nothing. I need no one to validate me. I need only to open up, accept God's guidance, love myself and give my love to everyone I meet. To create beauty in everything I do."

who am I?

Contemplations...

3) embracing the snow

10-20-97

Hello, Spirit. It's now Monday the 20th. I haven't exactly been writing this in sequential days. I have been very tired. This is bringing up all my issues of separation, rejection, self-worth, and so forth. Yet, I am ready to proceed. I will say a little prayer and then please tell us about the snow.

Good morning, my dearest Bill. I see you are having fun with your new-found career. Well, we all rejoice that you have come to be with us. So, please enjoy and play in the love of the Light.

Yes, the snow. You thought it was some acronym for sex! Well, I know we all want to get to that juicy stuff. That will be in the next chapter. For now, I want you to embrace snow as a term of change, a transition where water changes into a solid and then melts over time back to water. Snow: the sign of winter and change. Snow: the sign of going inside for inner hibernation and rejuvenation before the Spring.

I say this to you, Willy, as you hear me today. How glorious it is when the seasons change, when the trees change color and drop their leaves, when all of nature shifts to accommodate a beautiful ebb and flow—like the very breaths we take.

I am startled. What does this have to do with snow, per se?

Snow is something you love to play in. We have forgotten on the Earth plane to embrace the snow, to love its beautiful flakes of perfection. We don't frolic in it enough. We chase the heat all the time and move to the beach!

I say, a man or woman on this planet can learn a lifetime of inner development by tuning into the snows of our life. Pay attention to the subtle forces in nature as they shift, and shift with them. When it snows— play, play, play. Embrace it with all the glee you can imagine. Run, jump, belly flop, take off your hardened attitudes, and dive into it all. Do this with all the supposed events you don't want: play in it, make snow men out of it, rejoice in the discriminations it teaches you—like when someone says *no*! Laugh through it all!

What I am preparing you for is another fascinating lesson in "stick" philosophy, from another perspective. Nature is a place we all love. As people attune to it—its colors, beauty, and fluctuations—they understand their own process at such a deeper level. All the indigenous native tribes who lived off the land before civilization got so-called "civilized," have much to teach us about the Mother Earth.

I will not give you a discourse on Native tribal symbols, animals, philosophy, and preservation, for there are souls on the Earth plane who can spend many hours taking you there. What I do say is that a soul in tune to the Mother Earth is a soul understanding himself. The Earth is a larger piece of the universal body of God (me). It is as if each person were brain cells, and the Earth were the brain. By listening to the vibrations of the brain, the cell deciphers a deeper plane of self. It discovers who it is and how it lives in the greater picture of life. As the cell does this, it understands how all its brother cells must stay in union so that the total brain is healthy. All are dependent on each other to make the whole work. Yes, dependent—that word you all love to hate.

And such is the Earth. It is our compass to our own spiritual union with each other. As we pay attention to it, love it, listen to it, play in the snow and appreciate how we live in it, we learn the synchronistic dependence that each person has to each other and to the very planet we inhabit.

This cannot be overlooked. And note my friends, I am not here to advocate a particular type of activism, or save the whales as such. Much of what we try to save doesn't need saving. We need to save our alienation from each other, from spirit and the planet. As we connect with the Earth, she becomes a very trusted friend, a friend who can teach us much about what we currently fear in the urban jungle of protection. We cannot shelter ourselves from the snow! You can build a big house and lock yourself in, but the snow is still there calling to you to listen. Listen to the cold. Listen to the needs of the planet and of yourself.

Okay, slow down. One minute we're talking about playing in the snow, then we're on an Indian reservation talking about listening to the Earth, and now we're building a house to shield us from the snow. What are you trying to say? Why do these words come out so fast and so disjointed?

Relax, my friend. This is not Shakespeare. This is flow. *Flow.* Those who are guided to read will follow just perfectly. The bouncing around, so to speak, is an old brain technique to keep you focused and laughing. The more one needs anything to conform to some "image," the more they will be disappointed with this book and anything that will serve their highest good. The goodies that nurture one are revolutionary, an extreme opposite of the "tick-tock" of society, which is stupidly perpetuating a mass mind-set of conformity and externality. I keep saying "externality" as a way of awakening one to how much of our power we give to others, authorities, bosses, etc. I say with enthusiasm— "*damn* the others!" The only way one is free to love is to get pissed off and scream, "I'm not gonna take it any more!" Get out and follow your soul.

Okay, God. I thought you were about peace, love and understanding—what's this "*damn* the others"?

Oh, thank you for noticing! Yes, it is always so wonderful to see the looks on the faces of those uptight religious folks when God comes out with a good obscenity. And so what? It is just a word. What makes it right or wrong? What I want you to embrace is an energy, an energy that says I will not be messed with—to hell with all that does not support love. This is not intended literally or as a curse on anyone. It is not intended to be said to anyone but you! It is a liberation for the mind that has been bent on conformity and people pleasing, and has been dying because it cannot do the unthinkable. It cannot stand up for itself, cannot get angry. It cannot be human. Hogwashola. Get angry, get human, get crazy, and take that energy to the light. A good "to hell with it" to the world of insanity can bring more awakening then saying the rosary rote, hour after hour with no heart. *Feel*! Get out of the mesmerization, out of the fear, out of the insanity of conforming to those so called "good" expectations that have been choking you. Revolt. Take on your own power and step into love. How's that for awakening? Shake your sandals of the dust and move on. You don't have to do what you think you have to. Ah, I feel so good now! To heaven with everyone!

Okay, I trust you. Wow. So, back to the snow. What you're saying is that by tuning into the Earth Mother, I can speed up my soul process of self-discovery?

Yes, now you're getting it. Can you see this book is like a dance? I confuse you, you ask questions, and we both dig through to a collaborative understanding. Yes, all creation is a collaboration. Thank God!

Yes, I have been sensing this after the first two chapters, this concept of acceptance and creation. Yet, so many of my friends ask, "How can I manifest what I want?" They send out an intention, "I want to win the lottery, to meet more wonderful people, to get married, to obtain or make this or that happen," and then...it doesn't happen. Is this the result of misusing a technique or is it that in some way I'm not supposed to get all that I want?

Hallelujah! Now we're getting to some meaty stuff—the old "why don't I get what I want" deal. You know we have to start these books off slowly so as not to frighten anyone. But, absolutely "yes" to your question. I mean once one understands that all acceptance and creation is a collaboration between spirit and Earth beings, one stops trying to be superman and do all the release work by him/herself. Look at all the collaboration that must occur in nature for there to be harmony: Earth and humans, animals and humans, therapist and patient, employer and employee, husband and wife, Guru and disciple, to name a few. Where do my Earth friends get the notion of being alone, cut off, like one needs to take it on by themselves? We must only listen to our own inner intuition to get out of the "should" mentality and collaborate with the holy spirit (the creative universal love energy). For help, find those pioneers before you who have done the work on themselves. Awakening is nothing more than one released person holding a hand out to another. That is why I say, be weary of those selling a bill of goods when they have no inner release. Get a sense of those with an agenda, and trust those who give off the light. *From here, getting what you want will come.* (more on this in Chapter 6)

I tell you, getting back to the snow deal, the ego-mind world lives for disconnection and separation. "It" tells you the snow is bad: "Get rid of it. Burn it. Melt it. Get a bigger shovel and remove it." "It" says it's you against the snow. The ego declares, "I will overcome you, you nasty snow." I say, what a joke! We are making an enemy of our friend. You cannot hate and destroy that which creates our very existence. If we kill the snow, the rain, the soil, what does one breathe, eat, and drink? So you see, we again must take the *step beyond* the "tick-tock" stick we hold, *chase after this brainwashed thing or avoid this brainwashed supposed bad thing* and leap to the God force with Godspeed. I like that—"God Speed." Who came up with that?

Well, God, I don't know. I bet you do. At any rate, where do we go from here?

Let me summarize. Our Earth brothers and sisters love summaries, cliff notes, *Reader's Digest*, the mini bibles, and so forth. Quite wise, really. Reading a million words gets terribly boring. The snow, on the other hand, is endlessly fascinating. A trillion snow flakes all looking alike, yet all uniquely different (kind of like you earthlings). I say this with affection, for we are one. Just remember this snow analogy, for it is more than any analogy. It is the foundation from which our subsistence and our release comes.

Friends, choose now to tap into the harmonic progression of nature; embrace the snow. Allow it to inspire your life, to give direction to your path. The snow will remind you that all the things you try to kill are the very things that keep you alive. Release the need to kill yourself, your brothers, your sisters, the oceans, the air, the planet. There can be no death of any brain cell without the whole brain shifting and mourning the loss. So, I beseech you, my friends. Please pay attention to this. Teach all others this in any way you deem best. Stop the insane chase to save the Earth, and, instead, save the humans whose fear and unconsciousness tries to kill innocent snow. We are all dependent. And, yet, as humans, the highest on the evolutionary cycle, all change (acceptance and creation) must begin with us. Please remember that each soul that awakens, in turn awakens 100 more and then the next, 200 more, and so on. It only takes a couple of revolutionists with the right focus to change the world. Just release false religion and embrace the collaboration of acceptance and creation.

So enough for today, you have a lot to digest. I send you many blessings. Go jump in a lake, or a bath tub, and prepare for a snow-ball-a-thon near you. If not, go into your freezer and make freezer balls. Now is the time to love ourselves, to reconnect to Earth, and, through her teachings, to save us all from unnecessary brain cancer. I love you, my friends. Please accept my prayer for your deepest, deepest healing and openness to accept all the blessings in and around you. Namaste. Peace to you. I'll see you tomorrow.

Okay, so long. Is there anything I need to do in the meantime?

Yes, go fly a kite and play a little. Each day you play, you help a hundred others play. Each day you *try* to get others to play, you stick your foot in your mouth. And shoe leather tastes awful. Amen, brother. Keep the spirit shaking. George.

Thoughts to play with:

No need to be superman or woman. Ask for help.

We are all connected; we are one. Collaborate. Flow.

Spend time with nature; watch, look, and listen.

Something to Do:

Go jump in a lake. Make a snowman. Plant a tree.

Attend a native workshop to learn about our Earth Mother.

Contemplations...

4) relationships that don't work

10-21-97

Hello, George. Good evening. I'm not sure I'll ever get used to this informality. At any rate, I find myself more and more resistant to writing each day. I know I have said this before, but I am doubting this process. How is it possible for you to write through me, to talk to me? How can I be sure that this isn't just my own overactive imagination, my own knowledge packaged for consumption? There are so many questions. The more you say, the more I don't know how this all will ever end. Yet, I look forward to your words this day. I know relationships will be fascinating.

Top of the evening to you, Willy. I have a question for you on this fine October evening. How do you feel when you receive this material?

I feel a combination of awe and doubt.

Yes, the awe is what?

It is this feeling of something coming through me. It is more clear than my own thought. It clarifies the very questions I have, that I could not have answered on my own.

Yes, Willy, this is a collaboration as I have told you. You ask, I confuse, and together we come to nirvana. Fun, huh?

Yes, I guess. I just don't know what to do. It is as if I want nothing to do with this. I just want you to write it on my screen, so I'll never have to answer anyone's questions about how this was possible.

Okay, so this is your doubt part. It keeps raising its nasty little head, doesn't it? Isn't it strange how this occurs when so many of our friends are on the brink of their greatest achievements? They want out. So, be a good warrior and choose *"not out"* instead. Let the process do the talking. Trust and allow the greatness of my word, of my directions, to guide us. When in doubt about collaboration, surrender it to me for a while and I'll build your faith. Deal, my friend?

Okay. This is weird, but I thank you for taking the time to support me.

Well, let's get on to the juicy stuff, shall we?

Okay, George. What can you tell us about "relationships that don't work"?

Willy, I'm so excited I can't stand it. This is the whole tamale. (Don't worry about spelling.)

You see, relationships are such a fascinating, scrumptious topic. I watch our friends struggle with this and run to the bookstores seeking help. This is why I have to keep fresh material on the shelves! The key is to apply the stick philosophy to our connection with others.

Okay. What do you mean?

I mean that our friends, that are unaware of awareness outside the stick, turn to the externalities of life to entertain their seething rage—the rage of disconnection and the abuses that stem from it. Thus, "When in doubt, find a distraction." This is the ego-mind's game. This is nothing new—drugs, food, sex, people. The mass of social and personal addictions can be directly linked to the socially brainwashed mind committed to separation (avoiding love). The mind that chases the "goodies" and avoids the "badies" ends up with a lot of poop—you know, a life full of crap. Why listen?

The question is, "How can one feel free and happy with a ball and chain around one's heart?" This is so painful to watch and, frankly, quite humorous. So many obsess over wanting others to like them, to love them, to take care of them, to conform to their expectations of them. It's like hitting someone over the head with a rule book laced with rage saying, "You better not screw up, buddy. I have a dream for us and if you mess it up you're dead!" I laugh out loud at this daily. Yet it is pitiful, the extent that we go to not open up to the alternative.

And that is...?

Okay, Willy, relax a little; I know this is hard for you. Your back is tight and your scared. Please take it easy. It is okay to learn and be a channel. It's no big deal. You're just doing what your asked to do. So, please, allow the energy to pass through and let the words flow. Thanks, Buddy!

Okay.

The crux of the situation, if I may use that term, is that we are using the stick as a crutch and the crutch is "relationships." We want "them" to take away the pains that life has inflicted on us, to make things better, since we know no way of doing so by ourselves. And, of course, this seems so logical to the mind—the romance novels support the chase.

I say to you, repent from the evil chase and step up to the love. Hold the stick, laugh at it, and move on to the path of love. Love, love, love— just sing those great Beatle tunes. Hey, have some fun. This isn't brain surgery. This is a joke—a funny cosmic experience that you wanted to have. So, get tough and get on the healing bandwagon.

I say to each of my brothers and sisters reading, the only way to a heavenly relationship with others is to accept and create.

Now to do so, similar to what we alluded to in the opening chapters, we accept by de-stressing—working through our collective inner traumas (with help) to self-realization. I say, until you discover who you are, you attract all kinds of cosmic comedy into your life. The people you all have dated are quite the lark. Yes, I know there is pain. Yet, the pain is all of separation—separation from you. This can be resolved as of today. Please join the angels in declaring the only relationship of concern is the relationship with your own divine, the God within. As you awaken to you, a vital part of the heavenly body, you begin to open the path to healing the hurt and creating wonderful powerful connection with lightworkers on the wave you are on. This is magical and more rewarding than words can portray.

So, my sweet, dear friends, seek what is true in these words. Please have the courage to do whatever you must to de-stress and self-discover. Along this path of self-discovery, acceptance is key—acceptance of your life, of your hurt, of your emotions. Through your acceptance work you will find your lifelong friends, your spiritual brothers and sisters. *And this is all there is.* Once you have cleared your first layers, you awaken to the creative collaboration, just as we are in this book. I create with you, and when you are ready, you will create in many ways with other dear, kindred souls. Some may be spouses or partners, others sexual liaisons, and others teachers and guides. Let the exchange begin. Allow yourself the beauty of the wonderful spiritual flow of divine friendship.

I say to you (I like this phrase, don't I?) that there is no love but brotherly love. There is no romance—only brotherly/sisterly romance. There is no infatuation, or lust. There are no levels. There is only the heart that has opened, loving the exchange, the giving and receiving with another. Or there is the heart that is closed with the fearful mind taking over. (Please note: the brain is our friend—we do not hate it for following orders. We only seek a new order to listen to.) Even the mother who loves her child is in equal exchange, in a brotherly/sisterly relationship. So my friends, drop the soap operas and take it on—the real thing.

Wow, my back hurts now! Ouch!

It's okay, Willy. This stuff strikes a chord with you, doesn't it? The old backdoor to the heart....

I want you to know that this is the foundation. From here, we will jump into many derivations of relationships, whatever you want to talk about.

George, can I ask you a tangent question? Why is it that so many (now and at the time of Jesus) always ask for proof of your omniscience, for proof that you are what you say? And why is it that Jesus so often declined these challenges of proof?

Nice question, but it has nothing to do with the sex, obsession, neurosis, and the "wow" you seek, but I'll answer because it is relevant. The burden of proof is never on the master creator. It is always on the back of those asking the doubting questions. What good would it do for me to beat one in a game of trivial pursuit and dazzle with my great knowledge of now and later? Will that make one more apt to accept and create? Will that stretch the soul by listening to the confounds of a guilty mind that believes in nothing but hate? I say to you, feel what is right, feel what is love. All else is a concoction of soda water floating around, seeking its own self-inflation. This is where I plead with souls to drop the trivial pursuit and embrace the *Godspell*. The proof is in the pudding of trusting oneself, to know what is true inside regardless of the outside. This is what makes the soul soar. This is the faith that moves mountains, the knowing who you really are without someone floating down and branding it on your brain, that you won't believe anyway. The muscles of courage, the muscles of the soul, come from the freedom to believe in truth when doubt is all around. The proof is in what feels best. Only you know. Experiment and see. Does love feel right? Do the words I say ring true to you in experience, or would you like for me to tell you when the next snowball will hit you? You decide. The only way to know you are God is to trust that you are!

31

Okay, that was interesting. I guess that answers it. Let's go back to re-lationships. What is it exactly that messes them up?

What messes up relationships is one thing and one thing only: the pursuit of "specialness" in another, the very specialness one wished he (or she) had for himself. Thus, we project on the other a surreal perfection, and then we chase after their perfection only to discover they poop like we do. Then we say, "Neigh, you ugly fowl, I need another chase agent. Let me try this fine handsome lad over here." So we chase the images of beauty, money, success, and all trappings that we wish we were, only to find out we have traded our womb for a deluxe apartment in the sky with no love. Ah, yes, it is exhausting to seek "without" what is not within—a terribly comic game of blame, hate, ridicule, and upset that leaves one more depressed then when they first started. The rage booms. The separation continues.

I ask each of you, my friends, to stop this insanity. Leave people alone. Love them instead. Be their friend in heaven. As you have experienced yourself, Willy, as you have healed your pain and estrangement, love emerges naturally from self-love. This is the same self-love that says "I am important enough to heal!"

Loving one another is nothing more than allowing them to be exactly who they are, poop and all. And once you realize this, the ego-mind has a tantrum that there are no more Johnny Wonderfuls. Instead, we discover we are each so wonderful…. It is mesmerizing. Yes, the ego will throw a tantrum—so what? Our acceptance of our brother's humanity is our release from our own hell. Then the choice simply is, "Who do I feel like accepting and creating with? Who do I want to play with today?" If they are on the path with you, and there is love, then get on with it—have lots of friends of both sexes and styles, and live it up! Those who have tried and explored can tell you the great reward of soulful brotherly/sisterly love. The deeper you take it, the more you raise the consciousness of the world. Amen.

What about others who I don't jive with? Certainly, I don't ignore or hate them. How do I relate?

No, you love them. You spread love, prayer, and compassion to all the world. You help anyone who asks. As far as mates and confidants, you will naturally gravitate to those where this is an equal *loving* exchange. So, no worry. Be happy!

Okay, let me see if I follow. Spiritual friendship, drop the expectations and rule books, accept and create. Yes, I know this has been a theme. This is good, but what about sex, orgasm, homosexuality, alternative life-styles, and so forth? You have spoken of friendship, but what about romance?

Yes. Let's take these one at a time.

Romance:

Romance is the end result of loving someone deeply over time, through thick and thin. It's not negligees, candlelight, and music, per se. It's not getting what you think you want. It is a powerful desire to connect and share one's self, so that the self can be experienced. Enough said.

Homosexuality/alternative life-styles:

I tell you, this is a heavy place on the Earth plane. It has become a rebellion culture because of persecution. This is tragic. I say, whatever you want. Explore. There is no right or wrong, only love. If there is friendship and connection, be with that. If you are in a culture where a man has 1000 wives and there is love, I bless that. If you sleep with another person every other night, and there is love, Amen. Please drop the obsession with form and rights and wrongs. What you think is wrong begins a counterculture. If we just blessed all options, all paths to love, we would heal the planetary "tick-tock" ego insanity. All the "let's lock up these people for being weird" only creates more hate.

33

So, everything's cool by you?

Yes, of course, it's your life. Live it. The idea that some options are "better" than others comes from the rage of the ego-mind.

I'm not sure I can do anymore now. I'm losing you. Okay. One more…. Please do tell me about sex. I do want to understand the connection between the friendship soulfulness you profess and the sexual drive. I often wonder why we have such gut urges for sex with some versus others? And why the friendship love doesn't always trigger the sex urge? Explain.

Well, look at yourself, Billy O. Who do you love? You love the people who inspire you the most. Now, they may inspire your mind, your heart, you body, and so forth. There are many pieces. So if you are aroused in the genitals, it is because you are inspired to connect and create with that being. There are good energies to mix.

It's only our collective guilt that says sex is wrong, that this urge is wrong, and that "I can't because…" that drives everyone crazy.

What you really want to know is, "Why is there attraction, and how can I control it so I don't feel like an insane hormone?" Yes, this is funny! What a great problem to have! And, I tell you, the more acceptance and healing you allow, the more your sexual energy will explode. There will be sex all around you if you choose to accept it. (Ha-ha.)

I say, why not float with it? I will not give you a rule book. If you need to explore many sex experiences, do so consciously. If you are exploring monogamy, do so consciously. Whatever you feel is pulling you, explore it consciously. But, please, don't attempt to be a whale if you are a goldfish. When I say "consciously," I mean feel what is going on while it's happening. Learn from it. Does so-and-so uplift you? Or is this the ego-shadow you just can't resist? Let each experience help you make better discriminations around what feels right.

Most importantly, be what you are—embrace your nature. There is nothing more painful then seeing a homosexually natured person trying to be heterosexual, and so forth. *Be who you are.* There is love and friendship and connection for all natures. And as you honestly explore all options, you emerge to a place where none of it matters. You forget sex. You forget alternatives. You just love the brethren and seek to heal its hurting heart. This is the example of the saints. They don't have time for the mundane; they have time for the brethren. So, honor your edge of existence. Explore it thoroughly. It's like grammar school. If you don't go through each grade and learn what you came for, you'll need to go back and learn it later. There is no passing it by. So, enjoy.

Let's say a brief word about orgasm, since you asked. Orgasm is a physiological reaction to intense feeling on the etheric level. The more intense the connection, the feelings, the inspiration exchanged, the greater the release and joy. This is why one can have an orgasm and just feel like they had a cup of tea, while other orgasms feel like your soul was moved to heaven. Practice the loving friendship. Be intensely open and honest. Let your partner know your deepest fears. Let your acceptance and creation work together, and all of your days in heart and in sexual bond will be bliss.

Hence, the sexual response is in direct relation to our openness to feel. If we are shut down, we will not feel the bliss of orgasm. Practice. Orgasm is not a goal; it is a consequence of living in the truth with another. Enough, enjoy.

Willy, enough for now. I see your state. I want this to be joyous for you. Please relax. You have done no wrong. Please visit when you are feeling free and alive. This is no ordinary adventure. Please take care of you, our scared precious friend. Good night, my love.

Thank you. I'm hurting. Love to you.

Thoughts to play with:

> We are in rage because we feel separate.
>
> All abuse is from this separation.
>
> Release this through acceptance and creation.
>
> Love all as brothers and sisters.
>
> Drop the rule books and expectations.
>
> Accept.
>
> You attract who you are.
>
> *Feel.*
>
> There is no wrong. Whatever you want is blessed.

Something to Do:

> Whenever you are mad at a loved one, find a quiet spot, jump up and down fifty times, and scream, "I'm not going to take it anymore!" Then go for a quiet walk and decide to love your brother and sister exactly as they are. What you do after this is up to you....

Contemplations...

5) the saga continues
10-24-97

Good morning, George. I feel much better this morning. I watched this wonderful movie about Tibet last night. It was inspiring and also sad to see the suffering the Tibetan people have endured. Please tell me about inspiration and suffering in relationships.

Good morning to you, too, my dear Willy. Inspiration—what a wonderful word, like *Hukuna-Matata*. This again embraces the truth of our attractions to others. Of course, if one is still stuck at the stick level, they will find that their attractions will be dangerous. The mixing of energies with others at an ego-level will often worsen one's spiritual development. Yet, the "worsening" is essential to the "fed up" we spoke of earlier. So, it's all perfect!

Just remember, other souls are a mirror. As you realize who you are, you will see God in everyone's face. If you are in fear, you will see others as a solution to your problem, only to discover that they are scared and looking for solutions as you are.

The key message is once one has decided to be diligent in one's path to realization, then honoring attractions is vital. Those who inspire you mentally, physically, and spiritually are your brethren. They have a message for you. Often it will be all three that attract you. Listen.

The challenge is that human conditioning has made one attraction "okay," while the others are "not okay." Mental attraction is supported, while sexual/physical and spiritual attraction are dissuaded, if not forbidden. This is where all the sexual neurosis comes in. The reason is that these energies of creation are so powerful, so intensely God-like, that it has confused those not on the Godspell-realization path. Sex before realization can hurt you.

Yet, I say to you, repent from the repression of attractions. Honor them completely and manifest them in whatever matter calls to you. Follow your heart. Yes, there are times when you are sexually attracted to others when you are married, for example. Find your way through it. Be honest with all. Have the courage to explore what you are seeking, what inspires, and be with that fully, for if you run into the mind of guilt, the demon of darkness will forever keep you feeling alienated. Remember, the attraction and the inspiration is what gives rise to all relationship love. Sexual attraction is one form of this inspiration, where energies of two beings merge and create union, followed by the physical union. Finally, leading to the creation of a child—one of life's truest explosions of the creative energies mixing and manifesting a combo of both. We are all truly connected, aren't we?

Yes, I see. I guess I personally am struggling with sexual guilt. How can I honor the one I am in relationship with and honor the attractions with others? If they all inspire me, what can I do to prevent inner turmoil from the pickles this creates?

Pickles. Yes! I see. Loving all our brothers and sisters brings up all the most delicious jealousy and possession issues. I say, wouldn't it be a greater, higher place, sex or not, if we could love and connect with many more souls; to exchange and develop with more souls; to give and receive from more souls? Wouldn't the world just shift if we allowed more love on these many levels? If sex is a worry, indulge in it. What is it that you fear? That the karma police will beat you with a stick? You are already beating yourself with a stick. The planet is large, and there are many people reaching enlightenment through sex, through abstinence, through you name it. Just remember, what you have been taught to feel guilty about and have chosen to accept as bad is often the "accepted practice" in other lands. So, there is no right or wrong. Honor your beauty, your nature, your direction. What do you truly want, Willy?

I want peace, loving relationships, wonderful sexual connections. So am I admitting to myself that I want sex with more than one, but am I too horrified at the thought of the consequences to admit it? Could I hurt someone?

Willy, if you allowed yourself this path, you would be free. But in the meantime, you trap yourself with guilt and terror. You hang onto one feeling, that it is unsafe to leave the house. What does your soul call you to do?

I guess to follow my path. But, can I do both? Can I honor my girl-friend, wife, partner, and find a way to connect with other attractions spiritually that won't violate a sexual trust? Certainly there are concerns, legitimate ones: that it is unsafe to have sex with multiple partners and that, spiritually, it would leave you and the other scattered.

Well, there are two ways to look at this. It may get you scattered or it may get you more inspired. How will you know?

I don't know. I don't know if I like this tangent because it's getting too personal.

Willy, do what you want. Tell everyone what you want. Follow what you want. This is your path to self-realization.

Is this everyone's path?

Yes and no. Everyone has their own particular karmic cleansing to do. However, we all share the clearing of fear (acceptance) and sharing love (creating). You *know* the "acceptance and creation" life by now. Yet, the particular path, the way that acceptance and creation manifests, may differ. Some may need a thousand partners, others may marry at age 13 and stay that way for the duration of their incarnation. It makes no difference.

I guess I am feeling at this point that, even though I have these attractions, I really don't want to sleep with others. I want to have sexual connection without sexual intercourse and so forth. Is there a way to do this?

Yes, thank you. Now we are getting somewhere.

Please tell me what *you* think?

I guess it is possible to go deeper into the brotherly/sisterly love, to find some kind of sensual, spiritual touch, or something that makes the energies mix and inspire without "sex." Does this make sense?

Yes, and, of course, if you wanted to have sex, and these others on the same plane met you and agreed, it would be divine. However, what you are saying here is you really don't want that. This is a wonderful discrimination. You have experienced the fear and disjointedness of different pulls, and you know how separate you feel when you have sex with more than one person. So, again, follow your nature. It appears you are discovering it at a deeper level. Thank you for trusting yourself!

Yes. It appears so. I just have so many questions, fears, concerns. Who will I marry? Will I feel satisfied with one person? How do I deal with the urges for sex with others? Will I have relationship after relationship forever? Will it ever slow down? Can I depend on any stability? Can I get past my fears that someone will leave or die?

Yes, there are many questions. Just start by leaving the "right" or "wrong" behind and explore thoroughly. Let your own soul speak to you about what it needs, not the brainwashed mind. I believe you'll find yourself quite monogamous and quite the lover. Yes, you struggle with truth and free-love paradoxes. Why not explore both by having sex with only one? Try and see. If something else is needed, shift. Enjoy. Remember, lighten up. Keep doing your acceptance work. Release the guilt that keeps telling you, you are doing something wrong. The more you allow that guilt, the more the patterns of obsession and chase will continue. You know this. Stay disciplined and loving with yourself and others.

Let's take a five-minute break....

**George, thank you. This is a very emotional experience for me. I keep
having to stop and process and feel the stuff. Thank you.**

**Okay, we're back. Can we go through the rest of this chapter by just
going through the questions above one by one, keeping it simple?**
Yes, of course. I'll even bullet point it for you.

Who will I marry?
Whoever you want to—the core seems like an excellent choice. Get
to the core of the matter. Marry whomever you feel a complete harmony
with at the core level. There is no guidebook on how to feel. You just do.

Will I feel satisfied with one partner?
Yes, when you feel satisfied with you.

How do I deal with the urges for sex with others?
Become aware of the ramifications of your actions and always ask
what is the most loving thing for me, my partner, and this other person.
Let the light guide your actions. Release the "urges," which in your case
are nothing more than desires to run away from love—paradox, you see.
Sometimes the urge is taking you to inspiration, other times away. It's
just your healing issues.

Will I have relationship after relationship forever?
Yes. There are many people for you to meet and connect with, *and*
there will be one special soul with you as your partner. I say special not
in the *better than* sense, but in the sense that it is "okay" to have someone
who is your guru or main partner. They are special in your heart because
you are committed to deep work with them. Just remember that all are
special and deserving of love.

Will it ever slow down?

No.

Can I depend on any stability?

Yes, in your relationship with me. And in direct proportion to that, you will feel stability in all your earthly relations.

Can I get past my fears that someone will leave or die?

Yes. Remember *all is temporary* on the Earth plane. Remember to seek first the kingdom of God. Remember you fear what you have made wrong in the past. Someone leaving or dying was thought to be wrong. Make it acceptable that the universe takes the course it is taking. There will always be love all around you *and* frankly the soul is often strengthened in its love when these challenges occur. Please be compassionate with yourself and allow the mourning when someone leaves. Allow the hurt and allow the love in.

This brings us to our last point of this chapter. The question of suffering that you alluded to before. Why has Tibet been victimized? Why are women beaten, raped, and killed by their husbands or close confidants? Why is there so much cruelty between loved ones? And so forth....

I will start by saying the traditional domestic suffering that hurts us all is no more than a projection outward of the pain the "perpetrator" feels on the inside. The tremendous rage that has built from years of separation continues to bubble in this person. As this rage builds, the ones we are closest to feel the brunt of it in many ways. This is the planet screaming all around us for connection. The separation continues to hurt us, destroy us, and lead us to violence on one another. There is no way out of the suffering. There is only a path to unity, to love. I know this is not a complete answer to those in the suffering now. Please maintain your faith in love and your soul's process. I ask that each of us go deeper into the love process of acceptance and creation. Open your heart and pour blessings on those who are hurting, in little ways and in big, with simple prayers and a smile. We can embrace those who are raging from their eternal hell of separation and bring them, step by step, back to the light within.

This is the case with the suffering of the Tibetan people, the Irish, the Jews, the Native Americans, and many others, and why the most sacred peoples seem to be victimized the most. Who else would the raging people hurt but the most loving? They feel separate from the love and want to destroy those who do love. It is an insane reaction to being in hell. I say, please understand this. This does not in any way condone the victimization of women, the weak, the children, and the holy people. This just offers an explanation that gives hope that we can overcome this malady. Only by the strength of those who love, by embracing those in pain with prayers, innocence, and nonviolence, will love start permeating those who hate. This path must be followed with the utmost will and determination. I know once we look at our own rage we will understand the truth there. Please stay loving no matter who curses you. This seems difficult and unappealing in a million ways. This is *relationship*. We cannot have a harmonious "body" if one hates the places in them that are hurting and acting with rage. Only loving those parts will heal them. There is no other way. I send my blessings and all the angels with light speed to help you. God Bless. Amen.

Thank you, George; that was inspiring. But I still get mad that there is any pain, rage, and violence.

Yes, I know. I shed many a tear watching this. I can only say this is the nature of the planet seeking to purify itself. Any interference in this purification would be me controlling the world. The world cannot be controlled—it can only be *free*.

The price of this freedom is that love won't always be chosen or realized. From that choice does all pain emanate. So, love thyself and love your neighbor, for in the end there is no difference. Build your spirit and let your spirit's strength guide your way through the relationships on the

Earth. Union comes from the love of relationship. There is only one. Thank you for listening. I will go now. I am feeling sad and I need to rest.

I'm sorry, George. I didn't know you ever felt sad.

I do. I am like you. I will see you tomorrow, my dearest friend Willy. Much love and blessings on this most holy day. Be well.

Thoughts to play with:

Follow your inspiration.

Connect and talk to those you are attracted to—they have a message
for you.

Release the "shoulds" and the guilt, and follow your path.

Sex is a beautiful, sacred act. Enjoy it with those you love.

Allow your partner to be a friend, a confidant, a reflection.

Allow them to take you to Heaven. All of us go to God two by two.

Love your Ego.

Something to do:

Have a passionate love affair with yourself:

buy candles,

a fine wine,

make a sumptuous meal,

have a bubbly bath,

take a walk to a beautiful mountain.

Enjoy you.

Listen to your soul and embrace all the magnificence within you.

Scared Affirmation:

Thank you for coming to me my friend. Show me what you have for
me to learn today.

Contemplations...

the saga continues

6) why work when you can play

10-30-97

Dear George, good morning. I haven't visited in a couple of days—a lot happening. Yet, I am encouraged to keep moving forward to get this completed. Haste makes waste. I want to first ask about the concept of interconnection and solitude. After the last two chapters, I was left feeling, "Are we in this together or do we live life essentially alone?"

Good morning, Willy. There is no way to mess it up, so relax. I am overjoyed to be with you today, so let's get it on. I'll address this and then we'll move on to play.

The answer to your question is both. Life is essentially a relationship with yourself, and, in direct proportion to how well you do that, it is essentially a relationship with others. So there are two unfoldings happening: self-realization and dependence/relationship-realization. There are times of intense aloneness and times of intense relationship, and ebb and flow out of each. The trick, so to speak, is to realize that your self-realization comes from dependence and your dependence comes from self-realization.

Yes, I know you are not following, so let me restate this. Self-realization is one goal and interconnectedness with others is the other. They are both the same in truth, yet one is the inhale while the other is the exhale. Yes, many of our brothers and sisters are confused by this, "Should I meditate in the mountains alone for 50 years to find God, or immerse myself in serving and relating to others? " Why not both? Life has many paradoxes and this is the most foundational one. In life, one is alone *and* interconnected. It is in the alone that one grasps who they really are—the interconnectedness of it all. And it is in relationships that one grasps another level of the same—the dependence. So there is independence, dependence, interdependence, etc. So many words, all meaning that there are two sides to the coin and that is okay, that is glorious. The coin has a head and a tail. Accept and create.

Friends, spend time alone and with others. This way you will not be overly obsessed with conforming. You will learn to discriminate because the addiction to pleasing others will be released. Then, the truest love can emerge from realizing that you are dependent on you (the God within) and on all your brothers and sisters. Then, you can truly love your brother.

But this doesn't make sense. You have said before that we are all cells in the same body, and that the only way to change the world is to change yourself. How does this relate?

Yes, as I have said to you, if you want to teach play—play. You do it and 100 others you have never even met will do so as well. This is the deeper relationship. One does not even have to see another to have a relationship. This is the difference. Humans believe there has to be sex for there to be a relationship. Yet, you never see yourself physically touch me and I am your greatest relationship. You live the path alone, you relate to me as a brother who helps you along the way, and you pass that along, so to speak. This is the same for you along your daily life. You are essentially alone, and at the same time you have many brothers and sisters to help you with your healing. You do the same for others and so on. This can be holding someone's hand, or giving a call to someone in need—direct ways. Or it can be giving money to a church that helps others you never see, praying that helps others you've never met, and so on.

PS: The truth is you do touch me whenever you touch any creature.

So do you see the beautiful ebb and flow? Do you see the beautiful harmony in: 1) the self-realization, knowing that you really are a cell in the body of God; and 2) the relationship-realization, knowing that all your fellow brothers and sisters are in this body with you? Do you see that the only way through this life is *together*? The next step is how one is to best accomplish this. We will talk about this more in an upcoming chapter.

Are you following, Willy?

Yes, I think I hear you, and this helps clarify many things, like why I fear people. I guess I am still working on my own self-realization so that the relationship-realization can unfold.

Yes!

Well, how do we smoothly transition into "Why work when you can play?"

Willy, what do you think?

Well, I feel like this will be one of those discourses on how we all work too hard and that we should play instead.

Okay, how does that make you feel?

I feel bored. Like I could care less about any of this right now. I feel unwanted. Unpurposeful. That is why writing this pressures me so. I feel ego invested in my work.

Wonderful, this is therapy! Fabulous.

Willy, you are a magnificent child, as all our Earth brothers and sisters are. Please embrace this fully. You are wonderful because of *who* you are, not because of *what* you do. Yes, you have heard this a thousand times. I ask you to live it. The only thing that matters to you is what matters to you. This is part of the process above—self-realization. If, hypothetically, you allow yourself to go deeper into your daily process of release work, while you're doing your schooling, your work, and so forth, what will emerge?

I will discover who I am and what I love to do.

Yes, precisely! Stay with me now. This is fun. This is the very core of the acceptance and creation life-style. As we all dive deeper into de-stressing and release work (to love and accept ourselves), something magical emerges. The whole essence of how we live will start to shift. The whole structure of work, subsistence, and taking care of oneself will shift. Why is it that people work? To make money, to have some purpose, and so forth? Yet, the very place we go and spend 80% of our waking hours ends up to be a stress center, not a de-stress center. I say this, revolt from this! Find a way to subsist and feed your family that is nurturing and releasing. As each person does this, it opens up the opportunity for a whole new economic system to emerge: one based on love, fun, play, and helping, not stress. So, ha-ha Willy, you thought I was going to give one of those find a better job or change your attitude lectures. Well, there is such a bigger picture. Love is the acceptance of what is. Love is the creation of Heaven on Earth.

There is only one path here. Dive deeply into the path of self- and team-realization (that you are a child of God and that all our brothers and sisters are, too). Dive deeply into the shedding of the old and acceptance of the new. Listen to your heart guide you to the places of healing. As you make this your life priority, to the absolute dismissal of all else, of course, still work and make a living. Just let the metamorphosis begin. I predict that as you open the realization places inside yourself, the way you'll want to spend your time will shift as well. Work will now be healing work. This is it. Why try to do what you love and the money will follow? The higher principle is do what heals you and you will discover what is *fun*. Then, who cares what follows? Look at you, Willy. Over the past few years you have started to do more and more of "what is fun for you." You just didn't do this intellectually. You did it because you felt awful, because of a dedication to your own healing, shedding, realization, whatever you want to call it. Look at all the wonderful experiences you now embrace routinely. Look at the abundance that has followed. Where just a few years ago you were immersed in the three-piece suit world, where your spirit was dying. Now you play on the beach, bike, dance, sing, play. Now I say to you, as this continues, what will shift in the way you make a living?

Thank you, George, this is helping. I can see that I will have more joy in my life and others will be inspired by that. I find myself to be an inspirer, but not in the formal teaching sense. Yes, I will write and do a few workshops to pass your words along. But, more importantly, I have a life of fun and all that I do reflects this. I never want to be locked in to "a have-to" path. Whatever experiences I need to experience, I want to experience them and trust that there is always abundance for those seeking the kingdom of God first.

Amen, brother. Willy, you're the best! Now how do you feel?

I feel that for myself, and a lot of others, this brings up the real cardinal issue—trust. Yes, I have come a long way. Yet, I feel my trust wavering at times. I often want more money so I can travel and play more. I'm not sure how to create it. I certainly don't want to find a traditional job with stress, and so I shy away from such. Maybe I could meditate through the day and find a way to make any job pleasant. It just doesn't appeal to me. With this in mind, I say to myself, "How can I make more if I don't want to work?" The play I like. And right now things are working out. I'm getting by with some work that is stimulating. But what about the future? What can I do to make more, to support a family, and so forth? You know, I tell you every day!

Willy, you're quite entertaining. I think you have started to grasp the idea that you don't have to do what you think you have to do. So you're in a unique position. Not everyone has it as good as you. Bless yourself for all the good play—it has gotten you here. And, yes, there are many who are struggling with this in many forms.

I say this, wherever you are, consider different choices. Find more healing, find more play. Dive deep into this life-style. As you do, many new directions and many new options will emerge. Many exciting possibilities are available if you make this path your life. You say trust is a challenge. I say the alternative is to continue to live in fear, in a dull, stressed existence that you hate, but think you must do. Choose.

Let me tell you—there are no "shoulds." There is only what calls to your heart as something you yearn to do: art, music, theater, sculpture, biking, massage, computers, writing. Those who truly love and support you will encourage this. Take the "risk."

So, please, my brothers and sisters, let go. Now is the time. Forget a career. Forget the corporate ladder. Forget the economic structure, if it's making you miserable. Change it all, for it is killing the cells in God's body. Choose today to make the choice for your own healing. Make new choices. Dive in. Find the courage within to commit to your own play, knowing that all else is suffering. I promise you, as you stay steadfast to this path, though at times this will be difficult, a very new, joyous existence based on love, play, and joy will emerge. New experiences, new ways to work, new ways to support yourself will emerge. Remember, our deepest need is love. This is our purpose. The question is how can we live this, in work. First, forget the term *work*, for it is bastardized and the mere word makes people stress. Think play. Think outrageous. Think joy. Think acceptance and creation.

Okay, George, how can we sum this up? Are there any practical steps we can use to go from where we are to this new life? And, what is to happen to the economic structure that now exists? It has served us for hundreds of years. Does this mean capitalism is dying, or that working for money, that we then use to buy things, doesn't work?

Yes, Willy here are the steps:

- Commit to diving into self- and spirit-realization.
- Do whatever healing/shedding work you are attracted to.
- Let the rest unfold.
- As your release deepens and realizations emerge, allow yourself to develop hobbies that call to you—dancing, biking, writing, massage,

travel, creating, etc.—stuff you may have never done before or did when you were a child.

•From here, stay open to new life-style/career options. Do what has healed you, what is fun for you. Many brothers and sisters have followed this path and have gone from stressed out accountants to massage therapists, and so forth, not because they necessarily sought career counseling. They simply followed the healing of their pain. By opening themselves up with intense healing, a new way of life and a new way to make a living emerged. *Listen.*

I know many say "I can't." I have nine kids, a mortgage, etc. I say, you choose. You have freedom. You can! Most of all, you are here on this planet to heal the pain and embrace the joy. If you aren't participating in this fully, then you are sure to be hurting. I say this here, and in a million other books and sources. De-stress from the brainwashing; it is too painful not to! Hey, you don't need to wash your brain! And, remember, this does not mean quit your job tomorrow or that you will ever leave. Most will. Many will discover they are in the right place to learn and spread love. Let the light inside you guide.

As far as the economic structure and all the highfalutin terms you asked about, forget it. This is for the politicians and intellectuals to debate and waste time on. Who cares what you call it. It's just another revolution. There was the agricultural revolution, the industrial revolution, the information revolution; this is the God revolution, the Fun revolution. Nothing else matters. Joy is supreme. So heal, have more joy than you can stand, embrace the light of new options. Remember there are thousands of ways to live—some live in ashrams, some write best-sellers and live in mansions, some are social workers and don't care where they live, some are computer techies, others are nuns helping the poor, others quit there job and build a self-sufficient home with a farm in New Mexico, and still others will struggle where they are. Do what is fun for you!

And for those with doubt, fun is *never* destructive to others. It is only about dancing in the light of truth with God. Allow yourself some fun, won't you?

Enough for today, Willy. I'm going to do some surfing. Please have a joyous day. Make today, brothers and sisters, the day you start on the new journey to *peace*. My blessings. Mosseltof.

And, Willy, I ask a favor. Each day, or whenever you can, write down any questions on your mind and we'll address them as we go. I want this to start a theme. I ask that all readers send in your questions to some address at the end of the book. Future writings will address these questions and be written customized for the readers. Yahoo!

Thoughts to play with:

> I embrace self-realization (I am God) and relationship-realization
> (we are all God, dependent on each other).
> Work is an expression of creation, of the Holy Spirit within.
> Let your healing path awaken new hobbies.
> Trust—surrender to the powers taking you home.
> Abundance is having fun.
> Money is attracted to fun.

Something to do:

> Develop a hobby or rekindle an old hobby that uplifts your spirits.

Contemplations...

7) the adventures of brer rabbit

11-5-97

Good morning, George. I am home from yoga. I am tired, but feel free. Tell me about the adventures of Brer Rabbit.

Oh, good morning, little one. How is Willy today? All sorts of adventure around you, I see.

Today's discourse will be an expansion, the expansion necessary to enjoy the Earth plane. Everything we have talked about up to now is a prerequisite for this deeper understanding. In fact, unless our friends get a grip on self, relationships, work, and so forth, they often will not even raise their head long enough to look at this deeper concept of living.

The adventures of Brer Rabbit is captured in a song, a song you all have listened to. The song screams out in deep emotion—emotion of fear, insecurity, vulnerability, all the human frailties. The rabbit is small, weak, innocent. He was sent to this Earth and he feels alone. The rabbit suffers all the pains of separation.

The Brer Rabbit is the older brother, the older self that has transformed these frailties into love, adventure, anticipation, and outrageous fortune. In a sense, the Brer Rabbit is Brer, for he is a rare hare. He has seen all the fears and lives fully anyway. This is our lesson, too—the lesson of outrageous fortune: to laugh and step forward into the bliss that is all around each and every one of us.

Look at you, Willy. You are progressing nicely as a Brer. You have noticed that things are speeding up for you. The more you allow this, the more Brer you'll be. Let me explain. The adventure is in allowing each moment to drift into the next with an excited anticipation of a *miracle* about to hit you.

Remember the story of the Indian man? He, in his lonely life, one day discovered the power to create with his mind. He wished for a beautiful wife and, *puff*, there she was. Then he wished for a beautiful home to house his new family and, *puff*, it too appeared. One day the man thought, "This must be a demon doing this. This demon scares me, and I think he's going to eat me." And, *puff*, it was so.

The moral of this parable of life is the outrageous power of the mind to anticipate, think, imagine, and create. The only life worth living is *knowing that you have this power*. Whatever you affirm to yourself as lacking, missing, difficult, or unwanted, will appear. As is the converse. Anything that you affirm that is magical, beautiful, exhilarating, and miraculous will appear. The universe is speeding up, as is this power you have to create.

Yet, this power goes with great caution. Up to now, the universe didn't work its karmic ways so fast. If one had a hateful thought, it may be some time before that hateful thought attracted its experience. This allowed time between thought and experience for a change of mind, so that people wouldn't be instantly zapped by all their negative thoughts. This was necessary in the evolutionary development of man. Now the adventure goes on. The universe evolves. Time speeds up. The zapping, or the bliss, will occur much faster without delay. Now is the time to create thought habits that radiate love.

Thus, your mission, if you choose to accept it, is to be *Brer*—a bright, radiant, electronic receptor. Be a magnet that can create anything you want by the thought waves you send out. Choose wisely. If you find that you haven't manifested something, think of where you have cancelled it out with another "wish." Example: I want a million dollars *and*

I want what is best for me. It is possible that the money may not be best for you, so your soul will block its creation. This is just the tip of the iceberg, my friends; the miraculous powers of the mind have yet to be unleashed on the Earth plane. Most importantly, seek inner guidance on what to ask for....

Hence, I ask all my brothers and sisters to get out of the mud and jump into the pool of fun. Live the life of absolute love, fun, and joy. Do a back flip, jump into the lake. Do it! You do not have time for fear, pain, agony, and stress any longer. Your spirit and all your brothers' spirits depend on each of us transcending this negative pattern of anticipating the worst and getting it. Everything that has and will show up in your life, from your parents, to your life experiences, to where you live and what you do—are all the direct result of lifetimes of thought patterns.

Today, we all have the choice of choosing love, through acceptance and creation. Accept that you have made many poor choices with your freedom and accept that that's okay. You had the freedom and you made the choices because you wanted the experience. You wanted all the suffering and hurt. And now I say, please, brothers and sisters, the hour is near. Let heaven prevail *now*. With acceptance, love yourself, de-stress from the world and enter into the adventure of spirit. Make the choice.

Everything else is as I have said previously. Accept yourself completely—love your inanities and emotions. Take them to a healing source and release them, for you no longer need the pain. Release and let go of the thoughts that have kept you in pain. Accept your glory. Then go create the adventure of a lifetime. The Brer Rabbit adventure of the peaceful saint you are, overflowing with a lust for the spiritual adventure. A deep, irresistible craving for nothing but the truth, nothing but fun, nothing but peace you deserve. It is your choice. With courage and steadfast focus of mind, body, and spirit, each of you today can and will make the Brer choice. If you are here with these words, you are ready. Today, drop to your knees and pray to the God within, to your own spirit. Today, let go of the obsession and addiction to negativity. I beseech each of you—do not wait, as the angels are calling. It is your turn to return to the bliss, without delay. Haste no more. The kingdom of God is here. I love you, my children, my brothers and sisters. Take this day to be the last of pain and the first toward creating a new life of bliss habit, of absolutely committing to do whatever it takes to relax and enjoy. Allow your mind to bask in the juices of spiritual healing.

Please know that this choice does not guarantee life will get "easier," per se. There still may be worldly tasks to attend to: bills to pay, aging parents to care for, etc. This, too, can change with new choices, the choice to accept. What adopting the Brer mind does, is give the soul a sense of direction to God. Simply pray: "Thy will, spirit, not mine. Not my fears and emotions and charm leading me anymore. I give this to God and the angels. God's will be done." And, please, my friends, this is not designed to trigger fears of control. You have the choice *and* you are making the *only* choice that will bring you peace, love, and understanding. You are choosing love. Otherwise, by default, the fear rules the mind, and pain and suffering is your experience. I say, repent from the evil negativity that is driving you crazy. Pray a million times, "With love I accept and release my negative thoughts to the light; I need them no more. Today I accept the presence of God in my mind, body, and spirit as my guiding light. I choose to stand tall to discipline my mind through daily prayer, meditation, spiritual practice. Today I release myself from hell and embrace heaven. Amen." And so it is. Have fun; this is it. This is the transformation. Embrace the Godspell. Embrace each other. There is no time to wait. Heaven is here. With love and an open heart, release the old and accept the new.

Wow, I am moved. Thank you, God!

Willy, I say thank you for bringing these words to the page. You are a blessed soul and all the angels sing their praise for your courage. With each day, be an example of heaven, for you and all the world. Accept and create. Stay firm to your path. With this focus not to waiver from your single-minded purpose of bliss, your new life, your new adventure, begins. You have been given the key, each of you, to create whatever you want. As you stay in the Godspell energy by releasing all to the will of the divine—what you will receive is a billion times more wonderful than the childish Christmas list the ego would seek to fill. The material stuff will only bring you more suffering. Release it and find that life, as a Brer Rabbit offers miracles so magnificent that all the gold in the world would not touch its worth. So laugh, giggle, love, and embrace the Godspell. Never let it go. With the excitement of a newborn, embrace each moment as a miracle and look forward to the next with baited breath, for the next miracle to appear. One after another, they will appear by the power of our will, our power to choose the path of the Godspell in place of the pain.

Bless you, my brothers and sisters. Bless you. I look forward to playing with each of you each day. Praise to all the great ones—to each of us. Let us all sing in rejoice over this blessed day of release. The revelation begins.

Until tomorrow. I send you great blessings of adventure on your path. This is your sadhana, your path. Live it with gusto, with the power of optimism, for the miracles that are in your hands. Open your new eyes and see!

Jai to you, my beautiful friends. Jai to all opening their eyes. Jai to all those who live in the light. *Arevi Derci*. Amen.

Thoughts to play with:

Be aware of the magnetic power of your thoughts.

You create what you imagine.

There is nothing to fear.

Something to do:

Meditate through your day. Allow the meditative process to help you observe your thoughts. When you observe negativity, let it come up, look at it, and ask for a miracle. God, here it is; you take it. Cancel this insanity; I choose peace instead. Replace the family programming with God.

Contemplations...

8) when in doubt
11-11-97

Dear God, how are you today? It is a glorious Tuesday in November here in Encinitas. I look forward to our chat tonight.

Well, hello, Willy. We have a packed house tonight. All your guides and angels are here to cheer you on. So let us start with a big thank you to you. We bless this day and each day you spend with us. Amen.

George, I have compiled some questions. Why don't you tell us about doubt, and then we'll tackle the questions.

Sounds like a winning plan, Willy.

To start, I say hello to all my dear friends. I am so glad you are still with us. For without you, we are all incomplete. Please accept my love this holy day.

Let's get it on! Doubt—what a delicious word, so wonderful and confusing! What, why, how. Isn't that the way it goes? Questions, questions, questions—this is the path of western society today. It has reached a peak of analytical insanity to the point of explosion. Over the past 200 or so Earth years, the mind and its abilities have created more comforts, more advances, than all other times in history combined, and yet the soul is in more pain than ever. Why is this so? I say, that mind without spirit is dead. The "doubt" that I speak to you about here today is the mind running rampant without connection to the heart, and the soul. So, if the mind runs wildly unchecked, it will do what it has always done, create in the name of the ego—more better, bigger—everything but that which can bring peace.

The question then, is how do we stop asking questions? This sounds paradoxical, yet the ego lives on questions. It is always seeking and never satisfied. This is doubt. No matter what is obvious, the mind stuck on ego will cancel it out. I say progress is not progress if peace is not the goal. Thus, modern science is nothing more than a way of controlling the mind, so that it will create a never-ending flow of unanswerable questions— thus guaranteeing a persistent dis-ease with the present. The result is more doubt and more stress and never a time of peace.

I say, let go of this flow. Accept the peace of spirit and let the ego get another job. In other words, letting the ego continue on this way is like letting a steamship run with the motor as the captain. The motor only knows how to go. It doesn't stop to look at the stars to navigate a course. It simply runs. Hence, without the leadership of a spiritual truth, it runs in circles. More questions, and never answers. Full speed ahead, but to where?

And, please, do not look at this as an indictment of science. Science is wonderful when in the hands of those balanced and led by spirit, a soul that does not fall in love with words to the detriment of heart and higher guidance. On the contrary, in the hands of ego-guidance, more pain and world destruction will occur. So it is never the tool, as much as the con- sciousness, that is using them.

Let me get back to doubt, for this is the issue. Doubt is nothing more than the ego up to its tricks. The ego, by its very nature, is that small sep- arated self that is too scared to join with spirit. Its motto is "let the mind be master." Consequently, it will doubt anything beyond mind. It's other motto is "seek, but do not find." This is why some of our most educated Earth brothers and sisters are the most uneasy around spiritual or meta- physical reality. They use the mind to seek, but do not find. They ques- tion everything. How is there a God? Where does he live? How can we prove him? They go on and on with questions that their half-witted ego-mind is guaranteed never to allow them to see. This is because the science of ego-mind is always limited to the physical plane. Yet, these same people never "doubt" the ability of a TV or radio to submit a signal through invisible waves traveling through the air, or the airplane that flies with the wind in defiance of gravity, or the inoculation medicine that heals in defiance of laws of disease. These metaphysical miracles are everywhere, and these are just the base-level unseens. Friends, the whole Earth plane lives and moves in energy, energy that is disregarded by the mind. Yet, we know that when we are in dire circumstances, when the mind is forced to the side, we have felt certain energies (intuitions) save our lives.

My friends, I say, let doubt vanish and let faith and trust in reality rule your consciousness—the reality that is beyond the physical plane. This is the game that the human mind has set up. It creates a physical reality extrapolated on top of spiritual reality and is constantly mixing up the truth with the false reality. My word to you is live on Earth with a heart toward a way beyond it. This means imagine heaven and live it, right here, right now. Do whatever it takes for you and your loved ones to create this truth. Bring love to everything in spite of appearances. This is why the bible says, if your eyes cause you to sin it would be better to cut them out than to loose the kingdom of heaven. Now, please, refrain from hurting yourself. This is not about literal interpretations. Your senses are marvelous tools that bring depth to human experience. Just realize that what you see is not what you see! You only see what you want to! So, use faith and trust in the higher laws of love as the guiding light of your existence. Let the only question be, "How can I allow myself to love more deeply?" This is the path of Godspell.

Okay, George. I thought I had a question—but I would say you covered it already.

Just remember, Willy, to accept and create. Accept your mind and its thinking. Use it to cook dinner and invent toys. Then create—allow love to guide the mind to create inspiring works to solve human dilemmas. Let your life be a mastery of the physical. It is your gift, not your master. Use it as such. Let the power of love, the love that embraces all creation, guide you.

Let not the brainwashing control you. If you do, insanity will run your days. I tell you, more people kill in the name of something ridiculous, such as "what someone else said," than can ever be imagined. I say get new ears. If someone says, "Ego, blaaa-blaaa…," you say, "Cool, love, ha-ha…." And be on your way. What difference does it make to spirit what someone else's mouth is saying? That is their deal along their path. It is your response to hurdles such as these that will measure your speed through the game of life. And I mean *game*. It is simply a game of choice. And the only way to win, so to speak, is to know that there is one choice. Make the choice for the holy spirit inside you. Each and every second of each day, do not make a decision or plan or act or respond to anything without putting one hand on your heart and ask the one love question that makes sense—"Holy Spirit, what would you have me do?"

Listen and respond accordingly, for here is peace assured, and insanity and pain released. I bless you, my brothers and sisters, in your practice. Stay focused and let spirit lead you. In a short time, this spiritual guidance will remove your doubt and be a thousand times more rewarding, fun, and exciting than ego. This is freedom—using the magic genie when there is one to use, and enjoying the gifts given to those who dare to receive them.

Thank you, spirit. I will let all of what you said settle, for I don't know what to say. I'm kind of blown away. It cuts right to the heart of it.

Yes, it does. It's entirely simple. And for our Earth brothers with thousands of years of habit in mind, it is a challenge. The good news is that you would not have been incarnated now if you were not ready to take it to this final step. You can and you will, for you crave it in every cell. It takes incredible persistence to ignore God and live in ego. I say, each of you are incredibly stubborn, persistent, and disciplined. You have each proven you won't quit. Now, I say, make it easy and love. It's a million times easier than fighting, struggling, and feeling alone and dying.

Willy, let's get to some questions, for this may help tie together some loose ends. Let's go with the flow. Those who follow are ready.

Questions:

- **Can you tell me more about "accept and create," and how this relates to healing?**

Friends, there are so many words. This is part of the problem. If we had three words, we could embrace this easily. The challenge is there are needless words, and most of them illuminate painful existence.

The message of Godspell is a message of awakening. This may be called self-realization, or bliss, or enlightenment. It is the embracing of who you really are and living that daily. The path to this place that already exists, and is already your natural born right, is called "healing." You may call it other things, but it means helping the soul embrace itself and its place in the cosmos. The tools you have to get this are "accept and create." These two words help save thousands of words. For if you embrace the truth of these two, then every healing path has been touched.

The answer to your question is that acceptance and creation are your steps to awakening. They are your healing. They mean accept your mind, your fears, and your human insanities completely. From this acceptance, allow yourself to embrace therapies that will offer you the opportunity to release the brainwashing of the ages that brings you pain. These methods have been examined previously. From here, your natural creative spiritual state will emerge. Your natural cosmic humor, your love, will flow to everything you come near. This is the healing path to awakening.

- **Why is there so much childhood trauma and how does it relate to healing?**

Childhood is the opportunity to be vulnerable. It is the chance to build your healing agenda. What this means is the soul has a journey, and it sets forth to accomplish this by choosing a very specific set of parents, circumstances, and events that will bring up what the soul needs to experience.

I sense that the question is hinting at why are children treated so poorly. The answer is two parts. Yes, more love is needed in all relationships and, two, the soul called for its experience so there is no one to blame. There never is. Both parties, the supposed "victim" and the supposed "perpetrator," are interacting in exactly the way called on by both. This will end as the soul "learns" that this path of education is harmful and releases to find and accept a more loving path—the one of spirit. When the individual awakens, and commits to love by healing itself, its karmic pattern will cease to need pain to awaken it. Try it for yourself.

- **What is forgiveness, and what role does it play in our healing?**

Thank you for asking about forgiveness. I have chosen not to use the term forgiveness here for I am seeking new words that have less emotional baggage for our friends here. I can tell you that very few souls want to forgive. What the soul *is* willing to do is accept. Hence the path to true forgiveness is laced with acceptance, the acceptance that says my brother is not capable of doing anything to me. There is no need for my righteous overlooking of their great sin. There is no sin. He or she is playing their part perfectly, and if they're here with us we called them on. So, what is there to forgive? There is only the acceptance of the pain of the ego mindset and the desire to create love instead. This is not a contradiction to the poetry of the term used in *A Course In Miracles*. I say, this is just another way of embracing the same truth. So, accept your brothers and sisters, for they are on the same healing adventure as you. Each acceptance is energy that allows one to awaken.

Please do not confuse this with allowing oneself to be abused. As I have spoken before, there is nothing unspiritual about a little intensity in standing up for oneself. If you don't like something, get the hell out of it. Then accept and move on. Love requires that you take care of yourself first, so that you have something to give others. This is revolutionary. In direct proportion to the extent you give energy to truly loving yourself, true love for others emerges without effort or guilt. Try it and see.

• **What is a peaceful warrior?**

A warrior, peaceful or otherwise, is a soul on a mission—a mission to conquer the enemy. As the saying goes, "The enemy has come and it is us." Thus, the deepest spiritual meaning of warrior is one who tackles one's inner demons, one who protects the innocent and embraces the truth. How one does that is one's choice. The path is always an inner one.

Yet, the question always occurs: "What do we do about external 'enemies'?" First, heal yourself completely, and, if they're still out there, come see me. But what if there is a Hitler, or some maniac, killing millions? What can we do as spiritual warriors? Should we fight, protect ourselves, kill? The choice whether to be violent in this pursuit is always a controversial one, for if ego is in the picture, there is sure to be the desire to hurt one's brother. I say this, thou shall not kill. Yet, if there is a brother so lost on his way that he is killing innocent people by the thousands, restrain him, for he does not know what he does. This is a spiritual warrior's work at times, to restrain the insane from hurting the innocent. There are many paths to doing this other then the easy path of assassinating this brother. Yes, this is an option, rather then letting millions suffer in the hands of a soul so out of touch with itself. An obvious one would be to gather the community international and seek to arrest such a person for violating the laws of ethics and human civility. This is not easy, but certainly a worthwhile pursuit. Use your spirit to open to possibilities. If there are no other options, take the life of the one killing the innocent. This serves a higher karmic good. Yet, this is the most challenging task, because who is virtuous enough to make this decision? I say the international community needs to select an advisory board of a dozen living saints and spiritual leaders to help in such pursuits. This is deep love business, for love is needed to conquer this and many other diseases. And brothers and sisters, while these are some approaches, please allow the power of prayer to be your overwhelming guiding force. Please refrain from killing doctors who are performing duties requested of them simply because you disagree. This is why it takes great spiritual strength to know when to take one action or another and not be ruled by ego "righteousness."

- **How can we make an abundant living while maintaining our focus on spiritual practice?**

Yes, this makes sense. Right after the "What do we do about the serial killers?" is the question, "What can we do to make money?" Rather humorous. Truly, these are concerns, and they are acceptable as such. If one has a need to make an abundance, I say, why are you searching for what you already have? Who doesn't have abundance? The only block of such is the belief that such needs to be earned. Go back and read chapter 6. You have magnetic mind power. Allow this mind to resonate with spirit. When this has been accomplished, all abundance will radiate without effort. As long as one seeks without the harmony, they will run in circles and find that only one out of every thousand seeking fame and fortune get it through ego means. And of those, their lives are less then the poorest spiritual soul in healing. I say, seek first the kingdom of God, and all great gifts will be added unto you. This is the first, second, and last law of abundance. Be who you are, love completely, and watch. Already this is one of the obvious shifts in the spiritual world. Those who love are the most rewarded, prosperous, and joyful because they have it all.

- **What is the future?**

My friends, truly, the future is whatever you want it to be. It is completely up to you—pain or love. "Brer" your way through it!

Enough for this day. Have a blessed night. Praise to love. Jai to peace in each soul. Amen. Peace. Happy dreams to you.

And friends, when you have questions—meditate. Get on the computer and ask me. I will respond. Or, maybe, it's okay not to have answers!

Enjoy.

Thoughts to play with:

Stay positive, because doubt destroys.

You see what you want to see.

"Holy spirit, what would you have me do?"

Abundance is your natural inheritance—simply open to receive!

Something to Do:

Find a good therapist, book, or workshop to help with closed-eye visualizations. In your mind, release the barriers to your natural abundance and step forward into the garden of fun, peace, love, and understanding.

Contemplations...

9) *stay tuned*
11-24-97

Hello, George. It's Monday, the 24th. I am happy to be with you today. It is as if one lane has closed so another can open. I guess I will have to write if I want to connect with you, for my mind and my thoughts are blocking my meditations. So, good morning. Tell me what's up?

Well, good morning to you, and what a glorious day it is here in the kingdom. Glad you could make it. And for your meditation progress, maybe just allow yourself to be angry for a while. Consider dropping the holy act and be in the journaling. It will help.

Well, let's get on with the program. Let's get tuned, so we can stay tuned! I like this title to end the book, because it is hopeful. It is like that TV series that says, "Same bat channel, same bat time tomorrow—stay tuned." And like the TV, one must turn to the same station, the same wave, to get the same channel. This is the lesson for us today. That the human, like the radio, TV, and micro, is a wave of energy. Certain waves are in tune, while others are not.

What do you mean, wave? Like the ocean?

Yes, precisely. The ocean, the wind, all movement, all sound works on a wave that has a tune. To be in sychronicity with the energy waves of love, one must be in tune with it. To be in tune is everything. It is our hope. It is our way back to the divine within.

It is like a guitar or piano that, when "on key," makes beautiful music. No right or wrong, just the perfect tune. So, my brothers and sisters, today we embark on the final adventure. To tune ourselves with the divine. To embrace the beautiful music we make when we are tuned with spirit. Words for this are beyond comprehension, for there are no words to speak of the bliss that occurs when one allows themselves to tune in.

Well, okay. Where is this going?

Willy, you miss me, don't you? And, as always, you have a hard time receiving. This is what "tuned in" means. It is the absolute focus on being a love pitch-fork, love that can be given and received freely. Your Earth journey is the quest to return to this synchronicity. This is life—trying out all the pitches and sounds of the universe that don't work, until one releases the quest and simply lets their natural born sound ring true. This is consistent with all that we have shared about acceptance and creation, to violently disconnect from the pain of disharmony and allow one's self to be set free. So, my friends, do your work until you no longer need to. Then, like a fine instrument, allow yourself to be tuned every moment—so your tune is harmonious. Stay diligent on the path of virtuous fun. Accept the world, create heaven on Earth. Let freedom of the heart open to a new way of being. I tell you, the bliss that comes to those who live in tune with the universal vibration is beyond any pleasure one can experience through the limitations of the senses.

The question you all have is How? How can I tune in and stay tuned? Well, glad you asked. As thanksgiving emerges, the truth of the universal wave emerges. The thanks giving—the place in our hearts that is eternally grateful for its birth, for an opportunity to live in God's beauty. When the soul can honestly grasp this, beyond all the tragedy and suffering of the Earth plane, to sincerely thank the spirit for every moment, for every occurrence, as perfect for the soul's unfoldment—this very moment the spirit will shine to live a new life. There is no life like the gracious one. Grace in all forms arises from gratitude for God in the midst of all signs not to be. So, I say, love the Mother/Father with all your heart, seek first the kingdom of love and all things will be given unto you. Be eternally thankful. Give thanks to all you meet. Thank your brothers and sisters for their presence and their beauty, and their insanity and pain.

Bless all with a peace that knows God's spirit is protecting and guiding you perfectly. Please know that trust settles every problem. Trust says I don't know what the hell is going on, but somewhere, somehow, this is taking me home. I trust this unfolding and I am glad it is so. Thank you.

So, brothers and sisters, tune in to love. Allow yourself to feel gratitude every second of life. Practice this daily, so that in time there is no other practice. All other practices are to take you to this *one.* If meditation, prayer, yoga, and therapy do not lead the soul to live in love, peace, and eternal thanksgiving, then what use have they served? I say, let each moment be a party of love, an adventure in bliss. Be stronger than the drama of this Earth existence. Allow the God within you to emerge and know that you are way bigger, more powerful, more glorious than any adversity on this Earth. You are each the angel of love, bringing peace to the world by the vibration you live. So, my friends, my dear, loving friends, embrace this mission with all your hearts. Let *today* be the day you fall to your knees for the last time. Stay there in absolute awe, for the Father has spoken of your glorious return to him. This is the most blessed day of eternity. This is the day you are restored to faith. This is the day that you remember who you really are and why you came here— to rejoice in never-ending love and peace, to see just how much fun you can handle, and how much you can share.

The only obstacle is that we have been accustomed to feeling bad. The stress is so rampant, the illusion so thick, we have forgotten what a fun day would look like. I say, find your pitch. Find your inner tune that will make you sing to God in thanksgiving for each moment. If it takes a thousand years to strip away the illusion, it is worth it. For no other pursuit will taste as sweet. Nothing in existence is of greater worth than embracing one's own perfect tune, perfectly in sync with God, dancing through life and blessing others with this noble living. Please, my friends, do not haste. Let us all together fall to our knees this instant and pray to the angels and all the spirits to help us find our tune, to accept our joy, to live in tune. Whatever it takes, please let your love light shine. This day I say, thank you to each of you. For without each of you, my children, the kingdom doesn't exist. You are it. And, like a magical orchestra in the sky, all of us are waiting for the rest of the band to show up so we can make the sounds of heaven. Thank you, my friends. Let us join together, sing forever more.

Wow, George. I really feel it. You are making sense on a very deep level. So, are you saying that gratitude is the root to love? Gratitude is what tunes us in?

Yes, Willy. How can one love when they are pissed off? Look at yourself. You are a beautiful soul—a most wonderful being. The only block you have is this inner rage from lifetimes of abuse. We all have it. The only way to freedom is to let the rage out. To wholeheartedly complain, seek sympathy and joy, and let it heal. This does not mean wallow in self-pity. Quite the converse. It means, let the pain out so you will be free of it. In mind, body, and spirit, no one can fake gratitude and bliss. If we are starving and hurting, the pain takes over so that the consciousness can only seek ways to survive to ease the pain. I say, the way out of the pain is to pick it up, play with it, let it have its voice, let it scream, let it out so you will be free. Get to the other side so that you are free in your soul to feel good again. And my brothers and sisters, this is what therapy and stress centers are about. They are one soul helping another to let go of centuries of karmic pain from all the evils we have reeked on each other. This is just the truth. There is no blame. Blame only perpetuates the cycle. Fear is the cause, and the way out of fear is through the pain and into the gratitude of love. Now that's a sweet tune!

**Yes, thank you. But George, where does "healing" fit in? Are you say-
ing that the "healing" is the release of the anger, pain, and sadness
that has blocked us inside?**

Yes, exactly. Thank you, Willy. This is precisely it. Healing is only
healing if it helps the soul release the built-up pain. In mind, body, and
emotion, to let go of the terror that has shackled you. Yes, life has been a
dangerous experience through the eyes of these terrified filters of ego-
fear. Now we are at a glorious time in human evolution. We have the healing techniques. We simply must dive into them without reservation. We
must hold our pains, with a therapist holding one hand and an angel on
the other, and say, "God, I will overcome. I deserve better; I am better;
I am a child of God. Please release me." Any healer must heal in this way.
All true healing comes from tuning in to the Holy Spirit. Always pray for
the inner spirit to accept the healing of the Holy Spirit.

**Thank you, George. Is there anything else you would like to share? Is
there any tip you could offer us left-brain folks on how to get started
and how to stay with it?**

Yes, Willy. It's like watching a horror movie. You just have to keep
telling yourself it's not real. It's just make believe. Maintain your cosmic
sense of humor. If one gets caught up in all the devastation of the centuries, the fear will be insurmountable. If, on the other hand, you remember it's just a dream, then you will be willing to take the steps, to hold
hands with the healers and let the Holy Spirit in. Only God's highest angel can heal. Please remember this. Allow yourself to accept the Holy
Spirit's grace in whatever way you can. The earthly healer can only help
you come to a place of receptivity. The rest is a choice you make. The
choice to allow Her in. Please receive the Holy Spirit as the Divine Mother, totally unconditionally loving and totally powerful in her ability to
soothe any hurt. This is the step. When you are ready, the spirit will appear. When you want to heal your pain and truly live in gratitude, once
and for all, say so with all your heart, and the red carpet will be sent with
a million angels guiding you directly to where you need to go. So, again,

my friends, please don't haste. There is nothing for you in the illusion but more pain. Take today to write your own book. Journal to yourself on this path. Take note of your fantastic progress. Start today to unfold your mighty spirit. It is time to feel good again. Amen.

Oh, God, thank you. I have lived my whole life wanting to know you— wanting to feel your grace, and yet I have felt totally unworthy. I have felt so much anger at all the abuses of this world. I pray, "God, I accept your Holy Spirit into my being, into every cell and inch of me. Please release me from my torment. I want to be free. I want to live. I want joy always. I want to live close to you and perform my life with you. Please give me the strength, the love, and the guidance to finish my release and for the rest of my life unfold as you deem best."

George, I trust that with you all the fun and the joy that have escaped me will come my way. I pray for you and all my brothers. Thank You. Thank you. Thank you for your spirit. I pray that in some way my path may heal the world of its pain. Amen.
Again, thank you, George. I have been touched by you in a deep and penetrating way. I will never leave you. I may stupidly stray, but I will not leave. Give me the strength and the guides to keep me focused. I look forward to more time with you, in many ways, in all the moments ahead.

Great, Willy. I am happy for you. I accept your prayer and it is done. I say to you, and to all those with us, in these words: Go, enjoy. Do the work and *laugh*. Don't take this dream seriously. It's not real, *only* the love, joy, and fun are real. So, trust it is going your way. Blessings to you all. Go out and let it *be*. Let it be. Let the sunshine in. Love. Peace. Amen. Till we meet again—Namaste. Merry Christmas.

Thoughts to play with:

I am part of the universal energy.

Everyday I tune into this energy.

Gratitude is my pitchfork. It keeps me tuned to the love energy.

God is guiding me, helping me accept and create.

The Holy Spirit is God's healer. Simply ask.

It's all just a dream.

Something to do:

Find some quiet time every week to journal. Write all your emotions on paper. Let the rage wage on, complain, scream, curse, yell. Let the emotion out and let the Godspell in.

Contemplations...

epilogue

As I sit at my computer after the final editing, I feel a sense of awe and accomplishment. This has been a most unusual journey. I have been on an emotional roller coaster. Yet, I am glad. I feel free, free to be myself.

Again, I thank my friends and my dear Cori, who has supported me through this. I thank the various readers for their thoughts and questions. I thank you for spending this time with George and me. I thank George for showing up.

As I go, I offer an address for you to send your questions. I will talk with George and compile a list of answers. Let me know if you want your name included or we can use initials. Please remember that you can always get your own computer and ask George (or your own personal angel) for answers as well. She will respond. Many Blessings.

Farewell,

Bill

- To order books, contact:
Call 800.366.0264

- To send in questions, contact
Bill Jason
Godspell Books
Post Office Box 154
Cardiff by the Sea , CA 92007
- Bill is also available for speaking engagements and workshops.

"George"

**About
the
Author**

Bill Jason O'Mara, M.S. has been a pioneer in the spiritual growth movement for many years. He has been influenced by both Eastern and Western religious and philosophical traditions. Bill has an advanced degree in Psychology and holds a certification from Kripalu Center for Yoga as a holistic health teacher, and one from Robbins Research Institute in Neuro-Linguistic Programming. He has taught workshops all over the country on material related to Yoga, A Course in Miracles, The Celestine Prophecy and much more.

Today, he operates a firm called the Alpha Group, where he consults organizations on how to apply spiritual and psychological principles in the workplace and directs a yoga and health retreat center. Most of all he is a student, living a humble reflective life, awakening to the God within. Bill lives in Encinitas, California .

For more information on other books by
Granite Publishing, please call or write
to us for a free catallog.

800.366.0264

Granite Publishing, LLC
P.O. Box 1429
Columbus, North Carolina 28722